GOLF'S *greatest*
PRACTICAL JOKES

GOLF'S
greatest
PRACTICAL
JOKES

by CHRIS RODELL

ILLUSTRATIONS by S.BRITT

CHRONICLE BOOKS

First published in 2006 in U.S. by becker&mayer! LLC
Copyright © 2007 Chronicle Books
IIllustrations copyright © by S. britt

Manufactured in China

Library of Congress Control Number: 2005936147

ISBN: 0-8118-5774-3

Design: Megan Noller Holt
Editorial: Avra Romanowitz and Jenna Free
Production Coordination: Adrian Lucia
Product Development: Peter Schumacher
Project Management: Sheila Kamuda

10 9 8 7 6 5 4 3 2 1

Distributed in Canada by
Raincoast Books
9050 Shaughnessy Street
Vancouver, B.C. V6P 6E5

Chronicle Books
680 Second Street
San Francisco, CA 94107
www.chroniclebooks.com

This book was conceived, designed, and produced by
becker&mayer! Books
11010 Northup Way
Bellevue, Washington 98004

www.beckermayer.com

To **CHUCK MINCEY,**
the impractical joker

INTRODUCTION

GOLF IS A GAME OF SUCH GARGANTUAN pretensions, it's surprising no joker's ever snuck up on it and hung a giant "Kick Me!" sign on its back. Kick the USGA! Kick Ben Hogan! Kick the entire stodgy male membership of Augusta National! Kick the dour, glaring ghost of Ol' Tom Morris, a man whose every unsmiling picture looks as if it were taken in a room that smelled funny.

Those are just some of the culprits who are to blame for the enduring impression that golf is a yawning bore, a pursuit peopled by automatons whose trousers are more colorful than their occupants. A look at the game's creaky old ghosts would make one wonder why, according to the National Golf Foundation, did 30.3 million men, women, boys and girls spend more than $24.3 billion on a national golf addiction in 2004? And that figure doesn't count billions more in illicit wagers won and lost over who could drive it farther, clear a long lake, sink an impossible putt, or screw up the courage to ask the comely drink-cart girl for her phone number.

Few of those weekend golfers will ever enjoy the thrill of lining up a Sunday putt to win the Masters. For them, golf may be a diversion from a dead-end job, an unhappy marriage, sassy teenagers, mile-high gas prices, and that grinding malaise of a life unfulfilled.

In fact, when it's broken down to its primal essence, a day spent golfing is a diversion within a diversion. Tour pro Hank Kuehne suffers from attention deficit disorder and sums up the appeal of golf nicely when advising others battling the same symptoms to take up the game: "It's the perfect job, because you focus for twenty seconds and then you've got five minutes off to look at frogs and birds." Bingo. Think about it: The average weekend round takes about five hours. Of that time, only about twenty minutes is spent engaged in actual golf—swinging the club. The rest of the day allows ample time for hi-jinks, lo-jinks, and the kind of rampant tomfoolery that makes golf such a sublime parole from a life of toil and woe.

And the pity is that golfers as a whole will devote millions of dollars to instruction aimed at keeping a slice at bay, while few will try to divine ways that are guaranteed to electrify the fun of the game.

This is the first book that, if applied with ruthless efficiency, precise timing, and a face of choirboy innocence, will guarantee golfers a good time. Well, at least the golfer executing the prank will have a blast (warning: Some pranks involve explosives). This book is about practical jokes because that is the traditional name for a joke that involves planning, stunts, and a hapless victim. These jokes take it up a notch. These pranks can take years to deploy and involve thousands of dollars. They also share the potential for property damage and physical harm to the victim. These are impractical jokes. Some could cause the loss of friendships and fingers, get you thrown off the golf course, get you thrown in jail, and one or two might actually lead to eventual tee times in Hell.

Sometimes that's the price of a really good laugh.

The upside to those risks, too, is high. A good practical joke can so unnerve an opponent that his golf game will collapse like a tree without a trunk. So if you do wind up golfing in a foursome with Satan, Ghenghis Khan, and Caligula, at least have some change to rattle in your pocket while history's greatest monsters try to concentrate on sinking a crucial putt.

If you do wind up golfing in a
foursome with Satan, Ghenghis Khan,
and Caligula, at least have some change
to rattle in your pocket.

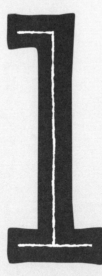

PRO PRANKS

THE ANNALS OF PROFESSIONAL GOLF PRACTICAL jokes are a desert so barren of true laughs that even diligent researchers struggle to snag rare anecdotes blowing like lonely tumbleweeds across the vast, humorless landscape. And there is good reason for that. The pampered pretty boys who make their posh livings on the PGA Tour have slavishly devoted their lives to being the best. Practical jokes can earn enemies and distract them from their duties. The reason they don't joke around is, for them, the same as why you don't see too many books called something like, *The Really Big Book of Brain Surgery Pranks*. For the pros, the game is a matter of life and death.

And it's a culture the snooty bluebloods at PGA Tour headquarters nurture. Examples of the Tour coming down on folk heroes like Chi Chi Rodriguez, Gary McCord, and John Daly, men who try to inject a little levity into the game, have been met with official sanctions and banishment. The lesson: These guys are serious...and so are we.

With so much at stake, one wonders why professional golfers would ever risk all to indulge in some playful pranks. Why?

Because it can be such malicious fun.

They waited until the
16th hole to tell the stooped
caddie what they'd done.

FULL LOAD

IT'S THE ON-COURSE EQUIVALENT OF CHINESE WATER torture. Taken individually, the drips don't register. It's the relentless accumulation of them that'll drive any golfer crazy. That's what happened during the 2003 Memorial Tournament practice round featuring Gary Koch, Curtis Strange, and Billy Andrade. The players and caddies decided to play a little trick on one of the caddies. Every time his back was turned away from his bag, one of the players or one of the caddies would take something out of their bag and slip it inside the other caddie's bag. Shortly after the turn, the caddie began complaining about how tired he was and how he'd never had so much trouble carrying his player's bag around the course.

They waited until the 16th hole to tell the stooped caddie what they'd done, a perfect example of exquisite timing, which allowed for two solid holes of mass ridicule. When he emptied his bag, among the things he found inside were four rainsuits and six dozen golf balls.

This would be a perfect story if, by chance, somebody had happened to bring along a small boat anchor.

A STICKY SITUATION

TEES, BALLS, DIVOT TOOL, SUPER GLUE—THOSE ARE some of the essentials you'll find in the golf bag of PGA Tour veteran Jeff "Seattle" Sluman. He uses the sticky stuff the way bakers use yeast: It's an essential ingredient to get a rise out of something you're cooking up.

Dudley Hart was flabbergasted at the 2002 Los Angeles Open to find his bag was quite the opposite of Open. Thanks to Sluman, Hart was participating in the Los Angeles Closed. Sluman had applied Super Glue to all but one of the zippers on Hart's commodious bag.

"I had to cut the bag open in order to get everything out," Hart recalls. "I wanted to kill him."

Not true, says Slu. "I did leave one pocket open so he could get to his golf balls," he protests. "That bag was still functional. What Dudley doesn't realize is that I was just attempting to look out for him. That bag of his was starting to look a little ratty. He needed to get a new one in the worst way. Hey, he's a professional golfer. He has an image to uphold. I didn't want him to go out there and embarrass himself with some ugly, worn-out bag. Geez,

I was just trying to do the guy a favor. What an ingrate."

Hart had just better hope he never shows up at the course looking a little worn-out himself. Sluman could be lurking.

CALLING DR. GRETZKY

IT TAKES MORE THAN THREE SUPERSTAR ATHLETES TO beat Canadian golf sensation Mike Weir: It takes cunning. Weir was scheduled to play a best-ball tournament against NHL hockey greats Wayne Gretzky, Brett Hull, and Joe Sakic at a distant Nova Scotia charity event. Weir arrived weary and complaining about a long day of tedious travel.

The Great Gretzky knew just what to do.

"I called the front desk and told them I was Mike Weir's doctor," Gretzky said. "I said Mike had hit his head and suffered a concussion, and that we're worried about him falling into a deep sleep. I asked if they could ring his room every hour."

Weir showed up the next morning groggy and irritated. Gretzky & Co. humbled the 2003 Masters champion by cruising to a six-stroke victory.

RATTLING THE GOLDEN BEAR

LEE TREVINO SHOCKED MANY IN THE GOLF WORLD with a lighthearted prank at one of the sport's most solemn spectacles, the Monday playoff versus Jack Nicklaus at the 1971 U.S. Open at historic Merion. There, with all of golf watching, Trevino pulled a rubber snake out of his bag and tossed it to Nicklaus!

Nicklaus, however, wasn't rattled by the rubber. He chuckled and tossed it back.

Or was the prank more effective than The Golden Bear let on? He was off his game, and Trevino became the only man to ever beat Nicklaus in a playoff. Trevino didn't think the prank was what did it. "It takes more than a rubber snake to scare a Golden Bear," he said.

SHIPS AHOY!

TOMMY ARMOUR III AND GREG NORMAN DECLARED war on the so-called Curtis Strange Navy at a 1990 tournament at Kingsmills. The "Navy" consisted of a group of raucous Strange supporters aboard two dozen boats anchored on the James River off the 17th hole.

"We didn't know what kind of reaction it would get, but we had an idea," said Armour. "We talked about it at the tee and when we finished putting, we went to our bags and just started launching balls. People were scrambling everywhere to get those balls," Armour said. "They were literally leaping off the boats. Greg and I threw about eight balls each into the water. We had a blast."

VA-VA VOOM!

YOU MIGHT FIND IT WORTHWHILE TO HIRE A BEAUTIFUL caddie to carry your bag, drive your cart, or just softly whisper instructions in your ear. That's what European Tour player Christopher Hanell did. He partnered up with the lovely Maria Nymoen, soon dubbed "Two Stroke Penalty." It may sound like an unkind nickname, but it's really a compliment. The blond Swedish beautician's good looks are so distracting that players who are paired with Hanell, it is said, automatically shoot two strokes more than they normally would. Wearing a short skirt never hurts—for either you or your caddie.

A PAYNEFUL PRANK

MANY SENTIMENTAL TEARS WERE SHED AT THE 2005 return to Pinehurst, site of the late Payne Stewart's memorable 1999 U.S. Open victory. But the maudlin atmosphere was mingled with some chagrin: Stewart's untimely death at the age of 42 left many PGA colleagues with scores to settle. Stewart was renowned and reviled as one of golf's greatest practical jokers. No unattended locker was safe. No equipment secure. No rodent roadkill free from being considered a prop in a prank.

David Feherty wrote in *Golf* magazine about the time he returned from a round to a posh La Quinta hotel room to find a groundhog poised to pounce on a place where no man wants a groundhog looking for his shadow. After some hysterical shrieking, in which the room's furniture took a savage beating, Feherty realized the groundhog wouldn't be seeing any shadows ever again. It was dead. And, it was wearing a pair of Feherty's underwear!

Just then, a knock came at the door. It was a maid holding a roll of toilet paper. Someone had called the front desk and said some was urgently needed in Feherty's room.

After some hysterical shrieking,
in which the room's furniture took
a savage beating, Feherty
realized the groundhog wouldn't be
seeing any shadows ever again.

"Over the years that followed, I tried several times without success to filch his keycard, but the best I could do was to hide his courtesy car in the woods," Feherty wrote, "an act made moot by his reaction, which was to steal mine and drive it back to the hotel, leaving me standing in the parking lot with my bag on my shoulder."

A DIVINE DISTRACTION

WARNING: SOME PRANKS INTENDED TO CREATE chaos will backfire.

Besides Tour titles, the fabled nannies Jesper Parnevik hired to watch his children were among the most coveted items on the PGA Tour. In several published polls among players, "Jesper's nannies" were named as the most beautiful wives/girlfriends/women on tour.

But like most of the titles, one of the nannies went to Tiger when, in 2002, he began dating Swedish beauty Elin Nordegren. In 2004, she became Mrs. Tiger Woods. The pair had been introduced by Jesper, who expressed considerable chagrin at the result.

"The original plan was to get Tiger distracted," he says, "but it hasn't seemed to work."

MONKEY MAN

WHEN JESPER PARNEVIK TOLD HIS WIFE, MIA, THAT he wasn't coming home until he won on Tour, she waited seven weeks then hired a man in a gorilla suit to serenade him on the practice range at the Riviera Country Club at the 2002 Nissan Open. The ape sang "Close to You" by the Carpenters with an accompaniment of fellow Tour pros and caddies. The rest of the players made a monkey out of Jesper, though, and he went winless for the eighth consecutive week.

OILS WELL THAT ENDS WELL

STEVE WILLIAMS HAS MADE A FORTUNE TOTING THE sticks for Tiger Woods, but few golf fans know he's an accomplished race-car driver in his native New Zealand. Sort of unfair, isn't it? He has two really, really cool jobs when most mopes never even get one. Then what is it about being Steve Williams that makes him so downright grumpy?

Of course, being grumpy puts a target on his back for practical jokers. In 2004, Williams signed a deal with Valvoline to wear their logo on his sleeve while he caddied for Woods. To get the grump's goat at the 2004 Ryder Cup Championships, the other eleven caddies and all twelve players, including Tiger, showed up for their team photo wearing Pennzoil patches for an oily dig.

THE OL' SWITCHEROO

JACK NICKLAUS APPROACHED THE FOGGED-IN postcard par three 16th green at Cypress Point thinking A-C-E, but left the green thinking A-S-S. During the Monday practice round of the 1987 AT&T Pebble Beach National Pro-Am, Richard Zokol and fellow Canadian Jim Nelford played ahead of the Golden Bear and Englishman Howard Clark.

After playing the hole, Zokol waited for a ball to land, scrambled onto the green, picked it up thinking it was Nicklaus's, and deposited it in the cup.

"There was a huge gallery following Nicklaus," Zokol says. "But when I picked up the ball, I realized it was Howard's, not Jack's, because Jack at the time was playing MacGregor and this ball was a Spalding. Well, I ran like hell off the green, and we were in the middle of the 17th fairway when we hear this huge roar. Here's Howard, playing one of the most famous holes in the world for the first time in the fog and thinking he made a hole-in-one."

Zokol left a note stuck in the ground for Clark at the 18th tee: "Welcome to the PGA Tour. Signed, The Crazy Canucks."

The joke backfired when it angered the Golden Bear, who'd been involved in a complicated bet. The Canadian tricksters had altered the meticulous score-keeping that would otherwise surely have led to Nicklaus winning whatever wager he'd made with his companion that day.

Mad at the moment, Nicklaus had warmed to the practical joke by Wednesday, when he gave a keynote speech to the Golf Writers Association of America. During the dinner, he told the story to big laughs.

"He wasn't too pleased when it happened," Zokol said. "But when he saw me on the practice green Thursday morning, he patted me on the shoulder and said, 'That was OK.'" The Crazy Canucks had dodged an angry Golden Bear swipe.

Kirk Triplett has surprised
galleries by pulling on a rubber mask
that looks like a smiling golf ball.

MASKED MAN

KIRK TRIPLETT DOESN'T LET THE SOBER WEIGHTINESS of competitive golf stop him from having fun. He's surprised galleries by pulling on a rubber mask that looks like a smiling golf ball, and one that smiles less frequently on a golf course—a Tiger Woods mask. "I would've had a hard time topping that (the Woods mask), but I had to do a little something," Triplett said with a laugh. "I saw this (ball) mask a while back and thought it would be perfect. Some guys were probably going, 'What an idiot.' I was just having a little fun."

TALL TALES

WISDOM WENT WITH THE WHITE WHISKERS WHEN old timer Sam Snead used to goad younger players into over-stretching their ability by telling them, "Why, when I was your age I used to hit my drive right over those trees." Always eager to snap up the legend's bait, the youths would attempt it and have the towering limbs bring the ball back down to earth. That's when Snead would say, "You know, those trees were a lot shorter when I was your age."

HOW DARE THEY?

COLIN MONTGOMERY'S PRINTED WHINE THAT HE'D never won a U.S. Open because he got bad tee times alerted the joker senses of Phil Mickelson. Montgomery griped he was always teeing off very early or very late. PGA Tour policy has strict rules about who tees off when because they want the most visible winners on TV during peak viewing periods.

Mickelson snagged some official PGA Tour letterhead, wrote the following note, and left it in Monty's locker:

Dear Colin,

After reading your comments in the newspaper, we at the PGA Tour Policy Board held an emergency meeting last night to discuss your concerns about these terrible tee times you've been receiving. We think we have a solution:

Win a (freaking) tournament!

Sincerely,
The PGA Tour Policy Board

The next morning, Mickelson observed Monty on the practice green muttering to his caddie, "I cannot believe they would send me such a letter!" Then he'd go back to putting and, again, back to his caddie to complain with bewilderment, "Can you imagine them doing that?"

Mickelson finally went over and asked if Monty had gotten the letter he'd sent.

HA! HA!

PHIL MICKELSON'S FIRST DESIGN EFFORT, THE magnificent Whisper Rock Golf Club in Scottsdale, Arizona, for which he collaborated with Gary Stephenson, gives hints as to what future Mickelson signature courses might entail. If the future holds anything like Whisper Rock, it ought to be a real funhouse. Several of the holes feature optical-illusion sand traps that peek up above what appears to be the green but, in fact, are nearly twenty yards from the putting surface.

Other elements reveal the prankster in Phil. The par five third hole features a three-foot, vertical-drop rock that has been dubbed the "ha-ha wall." The name comes from eighteenth-century English gardens and the reaction the garden tenders have when someone falls off the wall because they don't know it's there.

ALWAYS BRING A BADGE

IN 1992, IN WILMINGTON, DELAWARE, LPGA PLAYER KIM Bauer was told by police officers that she was under arrest. "They had me convinced that a van I loaned to a caddie had been involved in a hit-and-run accident," she recalled. After a while, they admitted it was payback from Nancy Lopez for a joke that Bauer had played on her. "Nancy was hiding behind a golf cart watching the whole thing," recalled Bauer.

MANHOLE MARKERS

ERNIE ELS WON THE 2003 SONY OPEN AFTER A second-hole playoff win over Aaron Baddeley, but Els is the first to admit that the outcome could have depended on a coin toss. Heads or tails, a coin nearly cost him the tournament. It happened on the 17th hole when Baddeley marked his three-foot putt with a clunky English pound. Baddeley asked Els if he needed the mark moved, but Els said no. His ball hit the mark and missed the cup. "I had to laugh at myself because it was just a total amateur mistake," Els said. "I should have had him move it. I mean, he was marking it with a freakin' English pound. The thing is about this high (one inch)."

We can learn a lot from a guy like Badds. If you don't have easy access to foreign coins, use a hubcap.

SACKED

FORMER SAN FRANCISCO 49ERS QUARTERBACK STEVE Young has faced down some mean hombres in his day, but one of the most stinging blows he was ever dealt was struck by a gentle 65-year-old known for wielding nothing meaner than a pencil. Young was playing at Pebble Beach one year during the AT&T Pebble Beach National Pro-Am with Johnny Miller and *Peanuts* creator Charles Schulz, who was 65 at the time and still a pretty fair golfer. The trio was waiting for the fairway to clear at the 15th when, as a way of small talk, Schulz blitzed the old QB from the blindside. "He said, 'You're really bad. That must be

embarrassing.' I thought nobody'd really noticed,"
Young said. "He ruined me. But that did give me the
incentive to really improve."

A BOVINE SHAME

IN 1934 AT ST. MARGARET'S-AT-CLIFFE GOLF CLUB, IN
Kent, England, W.J. Robinson, the club professional,
hit a drive on the 18th hole that resulted in hitting a
cow in the back of the head. When Robinson and his
playing partners reached the heifer, she was, amaz-
ingly, dead. No joke here. A pity, not because of the
cow, of course, but because of the squandered op-
portunity. A dead cow on a golf course that didn't
result in a raucous practical joke is a real waste. (See
A Payneful Prank on page 18.)

W.J. Robinson, the club
professional, hit a drive on the
18th hole that resulted in hitting a
cow in the back of the head.

2

TOOL KIT

LIKE AN EAGLE SCOUT COVERED WITH MERIT badges, a wise practical joker knows to be prepared. A good practical joker needs the tools, the time, and the mental agility to deploy a thought-out prank at a moment's notice. Here are some of the essentials:

MENTAL TOOLS

{1} CREATIVITY

Not only will creativity enliven your pranks, it will help you play better golf. Anyone who can devise a way to get a circus elephant (see page 90) to loosen its bowels between a golfer's birdie putt and the cup can certainly figure out a way to hit a ball around a small pine tree and onto the green.

{ 2 } A GREEDY ACCOMPLICE

Most really good pranks involve an outside agent, a foil who can lend credibility to an outlandish scenario that sets the trap. The perfect person for this role is someone who listens intently to the plot, chuckles mildly, and then says with cool detachment, "What's in it for me?" Greed is an important component in the perfect accomplice. A person who wants to be in on the joke just for laughs is apt to blow his role. With assured money or swag on the line, the accomplice now has a stake in the outcome, thus assuming an Oscar-worthy performance.

{ 3 } BOLDNESS

There are two types of people on the golf course: practical jokers and their victims. The stodgy victims will forever complain about the rascals who play what ought to be known as giggle golf to laugh and joke. By being bold, you can separate yourself from the pack. The classic film *Caddyshack*, of course, had it right. Just take a look at that movie and decide whose team you would want to be on: Judge Smails's or Ty Webb's?

{ 4 } RUTHLESSNESS

A really good practical joke can cost you treasured old friendships. But that's a small price to pay for a really good laugh and a story that will earn you more friendships than you'll ever lose. You have to be willing to risk the loss of a golfing buddy, not to mention your good reputation, for a good joke. Of course, the reputation you gain—that of a master jokester—will serve you far better in golf matches and lively companions than if you plodded along in life without risking friendships.

If you can conjure straight-faced
innocence when deploying your
prank, you'll hardly need to fib.
The look will sell the lie.

{ 5 } PSYCHIC CAPACITIES

Forget about learning to read the greens. If you can learn to read minds, your induction into the Practical Joker Hall of Fame is assured. The best pranks involve giving your golfer exactly what he wants. If he's a ball hawk willing to spend fifteen minutes in snake-infested woods to find an errant Pro V, target that aspect of his personality. If he fancies himself a ladies' man and flirts with the drink-cart girl, plan to involve her in the prank. Learn what makes your opponent tick, deftly exploit it, and he'll wind up walking straight into the swamp with a smile on his face. Divining the fragile vulnerabilities of your target will make your job easier.

{ 6 } THE FACE OF A CHOIR BOY

You may have bloodshot eyes, a pug nose, and scars like railroad ties across your forehead, but if you can conjure straight-faced innocence when deploying your prank, you'll hardly need to fib. The look will sell the lie. The best part, too, is that your victim will suspect you are lying but, being unable to prove it, will have to consider that you could be telling the truth. This will further infuriate.

{ 7 } PATIENCE, PATIENCE, PATIENCE

Revenge is a dish best served cold. The same goes for practical jokes, even the ones involving fire or scalding water. A really good prank is all about timing. Pull the trigger too soon and the zip, the punch, will lose its sting. Successful pranks need time to marinate. Think of how rewarding it will be when your victim, drenched in pond water, turns to you with a look of volcanic rage and hisses, "You must have been planning this one for a long, long time!"

{ 8 } AUDACITY

The bigger the prank, the better. You're more apt to pull off a really large caper than a tiny one with little payoff. The grander the scheme, the more likely it'll be believed and the richer the reward. Audacious pranks have an advantage: Even when someone begins to suspect something is amiss, he'll return to reason by saying, "No one would go to this much trouble..." right up until the clown hits him in the face with the pie.

PHYSICAL TOOLS

{1} WIRE CUTTERS

Golf-cart malfunctions that lead to runaway carts with wide-eyed drivers are always funny. One snip from some wire cutters can usually accomplish this.

{2} FISHING LINE

Thin, strong, practically invisible, it's as important to practical jokers as it is to the men and women who use it to catch fish.

{3} TWEEZERS

Scalded ball markers can't be touched with human hands. Picking up a ball marker that's been seared with a lighter can be too painful to bear. Try it with your buddy's and watch him find out.

{4} ZIPPO LIGHTER

One of the most important survival elements is fire. It's also an essential component in many practical jokes. When in doubt, burn, baby, burn.

{ 5 } FIRE EXTINGUISHER

No true prankster will ever want to extinguish a fire. Be it a golf cart, an opponent's bag, or his finely tailored trousers, it's always better to burn, baby, burn! But just the sight of a fire-engine-red fire extinguisher induces panic in otherwise sensible citizens. Running down the fairway with a fire extinguisher is bound to rattle your opponent. Emptying its contents on him head-to-toe in one drenching blast will certainly extinguish his competitive fires.

{ 6 } FLATHEAD TEES

That such a tiny peg of painted wood can provide so much surefire merriment is a tribute to the stubborn role of low-technology in modern golf. In a day when golf is ruled by titanium shafts, alloy club heads, and precise Core ratings, the wooden tee is practically Amish. It's simple, made of wood, and is usually given away for free in many clubhouses that charge for life-sustaining drinking water. That's why the flathead tee is among the most beloved pranks.

Running down the fairway
with a fire extinguisher is bound
to rattle your opponent.

Latrobe, Pennsylvania, golfer Tom Mueseler was victimized by one. "It was the middle of winter, and we'd just gotten off a plane in Myrtle Beach. It was cold, rainy, and that was making my bad back ache. We get to the first hole, and I don't have a tee. So I ask my buddies if anyone's got one. One guy says sure, reaches into his pocket, and tosses me one. I put it into the ground and set my ball on top. It falls off. I try again. It falls off again. Seven times I tried before I heard them laughing behind me. It was a flathead tee, impossible to set a ball on one. I was so damn mad, and that just made them laugh even harder."

If you run out of your supply or you can't find them in a novelty store, it's easy to make more. Simply sand down the rounded edges of any normal tee and apply a splash of paint to touch it up. Let dry. Carry in your pocket during all golf rounds, just in case.

"The guy who got me had been carrying one around for more than a year," says Mueseler.

Incidentally, Mueseler carries one around with him now, too. Once pranked by a flathead tee, everyone is eager to get even.

{ 7 } A BAG OF FIREPLACE ASHES

These gray little wonders can serve as multifaceted prank props. Fireplace ashes can be used to blind fellow golfers downwind, appear as otherworldly evidence of incineration, or reverentially pose as the cremains of a dearly departed loved one.

{ 8 } EXPLODING GOLF BALLS

Like a shot of seltzer water from a red-nosed circus clown, this one's as old as the whiskers on Ol' Tom Morris's beard. For years, the quality of the balls was such that it would only work on blind golfers. Thanks to technological advances researched by the thoughtful prank industry, today's exploding balls can fool even discerning golfers. While it may be hard to switch a golf ball on the tee or get a fellow golfer to ask for a replacement from your pocket, you might have good luck placing the exploding ball in a place where your intended victim may find it. That way, he will put it in his bag and use it without suspicion—and you can get away blame-free.

{ 9 } RUBBER SNAKE

Golfers are an inherently sissy bunch who consider things like gentle, moss-covered ponds "hazards." That's why something as simple as a dime-store rubber snake is guaranteed to liven up any round. Place it in the cart, in the cup—it doesn't really matter. It's bound to get someone shrieking.

{ 10 } SUPER GLUE

The Swiss Army knife of practical jokes, Super Glue can do it all. Champions Tour pro Jerry McGee tells of the time he saw a fellow golfer (McGee won't say who) get into an argument with a smart-aleck-locker-room attendant. Harsh words and threats were exchanged. Unbeknownst to either, McGee went into the pro's locker and Super Glued the player's shoe trees into his spikes.

"He went to put 'em on, and they wouldn't budge. They were stuck in there for good. He's still hot from his argument and then this: He goes storming over to the locker room attendant and just screams at him,

'How dare you? Who do you think you are?' The kid's completely blindsided by this and just starts giving it right back. I really thought they were going to come to blows. I just laughed my head off. If either one of them ever finds out I did it, they'll both come to kill me."

{ 11 } CHEAP PERFUME

A little eye-watering blast of "puff-fume" deployed early in a round can have as emasculating an effect on a golfer as a surgical castration. It can be silently sprayed on an unsuspecting golfer's back at any time during a round.

{ 12 } A STACK OF $20 BILLS

A palmed $20 will open doors of cooperation presidential pleas cannot secure. Always keep a spare $20 or two in your golf bag to bribe drink-cart girls, greens superintendents, or ethically carefree police officers. Fives and tens are chump change. It takes Andy Jackson to secure a faithful foil.

3

MINDLESS PRANKS
FOR MINDLESS FUN

 S WE'VE SEEN, PRACTICAL JOKES ARE LIKE A box full of crayons. They come in all sorts of colors. Some are beige and rather flavorless, while others pack the vivid punch of an Atomic Tangerine. A good practical joke can involve a cast of dozens, months of preparation, and the construction of elaborate sets. Others are simple vandalism—and that's not meant to disparage vandals and vandalism. The original Vandals were a fierce Germanic tribe that in the fifth century A.D. first began to trip up the Roman Empire (and anything that big that spends its entire time 'roamin' around was bound to tumble). They left no mark on culture, no monuments of their reign. And the only thing that resounds about the Vandals today is the nastiness associated with their name, which was derived from the fear and hatred felt toward them by African Catholics and a reminiscence of the time they sacked Rome. They were a brutal, destructive people and never gave any indication of any artistic bent. Ignorant of culture, bereft of thoughtfulness, the Vandals were a nasty scourge to budding civilizations aspiring to elevate the condition of mankind. But, hey, it's a pretty safe bet that they probably enjoyed a couple of good laughs while they were off destroying stuff.

PROP JOKES

Golf vandalism lets your inner Stooge out for a stroll. Just about any simple tool or device can be vandalized. Don't try to be creative or artistic. Remember: The original Vandals didn't put on any fancy airs. They just broke things. Let them be your inspiration.

DR. TEE

MANY JACKKNIFED TEES LITTER THE TEE BOXES OF golf courses across America. Pick up every broken one you can find and gently fold it back into place. It's easy and the tees will look like brand-new. Then put them all in your buddy's golf bag. It's a simple prank, but the tee will break easily when a golfer attempts to shove it into semi-hard ground. This will either annoy him because he'll have to mutter and go get another tee (cross your fingers it's another pre-broken one) or cause him severe pain, as some heavyset golfers are known to topple in a heap when a tee breaks while they're in that awkward position.

PUDDING CUP

SOME SIMPLE, DISGUSTING FUN FOR THE GROUP behind you. After you putt out, fill each cup with a different flavor of pudding. If, by chance, you run out and you're near a pasture with grazing livestock, be creative!

THE WORLD'S LARGEST DIVOT: YOUR CART PARTNER'S BAG

POOR ETIQUETTE IS THE RUIN OF GOLF. IF YOUR partner makes the common faux pas of failing to repair his dainty divot, teach him a lesson. Take the cart-mounted, quart-sized bottle of divot dust and empty the entire contents into the bag pocket where he keeps all his balls and tees. If you're fortunate enough to have a cart with two bottles, dump the sandy mix into the main compartment where all the clubs are kept. If you have enough, you ought to be able to fill it up enough to cover the grips—a real mess. If he gets angry, tell him it's impolite to not repair your divots.

CORN DIVOT

KEEP A SMALL SACK OF CORN KERNELS IN YOUR GOLF bag. If your opponent is the sort who takes long, sleek divots, jump out to retrieve and—"Shucks, I don't mind..."—repair it yourself. Before replacing the divot, put three Super-Stock/Fast-Gro corn kernels under the divot. Continue throughout the summer. Some corn will sprout, causing vexation among the local crew. Eventually report your opponent to the greens superintendent. Swear that you saw him do it multiple times and that your conscience dictates you finally come forward.

ENJOY A FAST BREAK

UNPROVOKED, REMOVE A CLUB FROM YOUR OPPO-nent's bag. Then snap it over your knee. He'll angrily ask why you would do such a malicious thing. Simply say, "'cause I felt like it." He'll respond, no doubt, with profane hostility, threats, and instructions about your further behavior. No matter what he says, reply, "You're not the boss of me!" Then get ready to run away laughing maniacally.

Before replacing the divot,
put three Super-Stock/Fast-Gro
corn kernels under the divot.
Continue throughout the summer.

FIRE ONE!

YOU'LL NEED TO WORK FAST AND EXPLOIT A PRECIOUS time when your ball markers are close together on the putting surface. But it'll only take about twenty seconds, so it can be done if done with deftness. While you're pretending to line up your own putt, take tweezers and a lighter and make your opponent's ball marker hotter than the surface of the sun.

LAST RESORT

IF ALL ELSE FAILS, EMBRACE THE SOLUTION THAT SAVED the caveman and allowed the perpetuation of our species. Light his bag on fire. Stand around and chant like a primitive as he tries to stomp it out.

HEAD GAMES

Arnold Palmer says the most important distance in golf is the few inches between your ears. It is a game of concentration and mental rigor. Maybe that's why some true dummies flourish at the sport. If you can't think very hard, you'll never appreciate just how difficult an undertaking golf is. But for those of us cursed with thoughtfulness, golf can be a nightmare. We think about swing thoughts, we think about matches, we think about pace of play, we think what we're doing is impossible. And it is—especially if you can find a way to add some chaos to the swing thoughts of the people you're eager to beat.

TEE OFF

IN EXCHANGE FOR THEIR SERVICES, PROMISE A POST-match round of beers for the group in front of you. Have them at first subtly move the tee markers in odd directions. It's jarring to have them pointing away from the hole even slightly. Then on one designated hole, have them point the markers completely in the wrong direction at a hole that might be the actual green but isn't.

Let your partner win the previous hole so he has the honor.

After his wildly errant drive, hit it down the correct fairway and call him an idiot. If he takes time to respond, warn him he'd better scramble after his ball or risk a two-stroke penalty.

MIND
CLUTTER

A CONSTANT STREAM OF INANE TRIVIA CAN HELP distract even focused golfers. Casually mention that noted golf historian Ben Crenshaw and his wife, Julie, have a cat named Francis. During their years together, they've also had cats named Ben and Bobby. Their full names of the felines are Francis Ouimet, Ben Hogan, and Bobby Jones. Inane trivia is wonderful.

But if you find yourself being victimized by a steady stream of mind-numbing golf minutiae such as the names of the Crenshaw cats, you can strike back by invoking the little-used Rule 33-7:

> *Any penalty less than disqualification must not be waived or modified. If a Committee considers that a player is guilty of a serious breach of etiquette, it may impose a penalty of disqualification under this Rule.*

This can be known as the "Talks-Too-Much" rule and covers severe etiquette violations such as intentionally offending or distracting another player. The great thing about it is, once it is invoked against an opponent, anything said in defense is, in effect, another violation. For instance, if your opponent begins protesting that he is not in violation, point out that his defense requires talking. If he says something else, interrupt with, "There you go again! Rule 33-7!"

CART QUIRKS

GOLF CARTS ARE LIKE THE GOLFERS THAT USE THEM: Each is an individual with its own personality. Some are strong, some are weak, some are plodding, and some are robust. None of these interest you. Find the one cart that doesn't urgently "Beeeep!" when it is shoved into reverse. Almost every golf course has one stricken with this malfunction too trifling to correct.

Always secure it for your group.

Then spend the round surreptitiously shifting it into reverse. Leave it parked in front of steep bunkers, hills, trees, sand traps, and water hazards so your cart partner will unwittingly have to move it while you're playing a shot far away.

Either way,
testosterone-infused golfers
will be distracted.

"DID YOU SEE THAT?"

MEN FIND IT HARD TO PAR THE SECOND HOLE AT THE Golf de Andraxt course in Mallorca. The 161-yard par three is quite small and next to one of comely supermodel Claudia Schiffer's houses. It's hard to see her because the house is "paparazzi-proofed," with towering walls and hedges obscuring prying lenses and eyes. But the possibility of seeing her is exciting, and you will always be reminded of her presence because the scorecard says the hole is called "Casa Claudia." Claudia herself plays golf once in a while.

Of course, you don't have to be playing someplace exotic for a distracting prank like this to work. You could say you've seen the local weather gal sunning herself on the porch or just say it was some sporty divorcée. Either way, testosterone-infused golfers will be distracted.

Even better, say you heard a friend say "she" often watches golfers from the window—nude—and has been known to invite particularly big hitters up to the porch for post-round libations.

Assure them it's just a rumor but, hey, did you just see that curtain move?

CHIPS AHOY!

TRUE: BEN CRENSHAW USES A DECIDEDLY LOW-TECH way to design championship greens like the ones the pros putt on at Kapalua Golf Club's Plantation Course in Hawaii: a bag of potato chips. Crenshaw was eating a bag of potato chips with the developers of the seaside resort when one of them asked what kind of computer program he uses to design the undulations of the greens. Crenshaw said he wouldn't dream of entrusting such calculations to a computer. Instead, he pulled out a chip from a bagful he was snacking on and said, "This is the 18th green." He proceeded to lay out the course using chips that had the breaks he wanted. The chips were later used as models for the actual greens he and Bill Coore designed.

You can use this interesting bit of true trivia to your advantage. Inform your opponent that your course was designed by a Crenshaw disciple who gave you the chips he used to design the greens. At each hole pull out a chip to study your own putt. Then graciously offer it to your opponent, but when he reaches out to study it, stuff it into your mouth, chomp it into pieces, and make a big show out of swallowing the entire chip. This will work great if you keep sinking all your putts.

A SNAPPY COMEBACK

MIKE PETERS IS THE AUTHOR AND ILLUSTRATOR behind the great *Mother Goose and Grimm* comic strip. In one strip, he writes about a golfer being kicked off the course for breaking sixty. "Sixty!" exclaims his partner. "That's incredible."

The other golfer replies, "I know. I never thought a golf cart could go that fast!"

That's a great ego-deflating line to remember any time your opponent comes out with a preposterous number for his scorecard.

STROLL, DON'T ROLL

BRAG TO YOUR OPPONENT ABOUT THE IMPORTANCE of walking, rather than riding. Then, once he agrees—shame him for sissiness if he refuses—spend the entire round beating the bushes for lost balls. For agreeing to walk in a gentlemanly game, tell him you'll give him every ball you find (scatter a dozen or so the previous night in nearby ball nests so you can up the ante). Most golfers can't refuse free golf balls, especially now that they're so expensive ball manufacturers qualify for OPEC membership. But you'll be surprised how much heavier a couple dozen golf balls makes an ordinary golf bag. This will make you look like a good guy while your opponent tires from carrying the heavy-duty bag. If this is too subtle for you, it's okay to resort to bricks or stones.

CHA-CHING! CHING! CHING!

IN A *GOLF* MAGAZINE SURVEY, PGA PLAYERS SAID THE numbskulled rattling of change and keys in a spectator's pocket is among the biggest distractions in tournament golf.

Try it. A few quarters, some nickels, and a chain of keys like the ones wielded by custodians employed by large office buildings ought to make enough of a racket. If someone gets offended, simply plead ignorance— "Hey, it's a habit! I don't even know when I'm doing it!"—and continue rattling away. By the end of the round, even your occasional silences will unnerve.

ALLER-GEEZ!

COMPLAIN BITTERLY ABOUT YOUR ALLERGIES AND then fake sneeze every single time your opponent draws his club back to strike the ball. Every single time. To be really effective, put a little water in the palm of your hand. When he draws his club back on an important drive, time your toss so it'll hit him a fraction of a second after you let loose with a supersonic sneeze. Aim for the back of his neck.

MOBILE FLAG

WHEN PLAYING A PAR THREE IN FRONT OF A GROUP of friends, demonstrate your utter contempt for their shotmaking abilities by standing around the flag with your backs turned toward the tee. Don't turn and wave. Don't joke. Just stand there like four cigar-store Indians, absolutely still.

If they are golfers of wit, upon hitting they will shout, "Fore! We mean it! Foooore! It's coming right at you!" But do not budge. They are lying.

Then be sure to move and stand with the flag someplace that is a significant distance from the actual hole location. Important: Make sure your about-face positions are about sixty feet from the hole and dangerously near an angry-looking hazard.

THE DISAPPEARING FLAG

SIMILAR TO MOBILE FLAG, BUT WITH LESS DARING and creative flair. Can be done on any hole by never replacing the flag after putting out. Simply leave it laying on the ground far, far away from the hole. Again, you must know the people behind you, or simply be out to infuriate strangers.

If trouble ensues, point out that they were missing the green anyway so you figured it wouldn't matter whether the pin was in or not.

STOP! THIEF!

WHEN YOU SEE THE DRINK-CART GIRL APPROACHING, quickly remove the keys from your cart and head to your ball on the far side of the fairway. As soon as his back is turned and the girl guns her cart to drive away, say, "Did you see that? She took something out of our cart!"

Walking with his bag over his
shoulder will give him a lot of time to
try to divine why a drink-cart girl
would steal your cart keys.

When he rushes back to your golf cart to investigate, he'll check his property and find it all there. Relieved, he'll reach for the keys to try and start the cart. But it will remain in a state of motionlessness. This will put him in a state of anger.

Walking with his bag over his shoulder will give him a lot of time to try to divine why a drink-cart girl would steal your cart keys. Sure, it won't be any fun for you carrying your bag either, but let his bitter complaints fuel your every step. The real fun will begin when he confronts the dumbfounded drink-cart girl over why she stole your cart keys.

CONSTRUCTION/ DESTRUCTION

Your opponents may spend hours at the practice range trying to score a practical advantage over you. You can render this a moot point by spending an equally dedicated amount of time in a workshop creating tools, weapons, and gags that will give you a matchless advantage over the most nimble-swinging golfer.

CLUBS AWAY!

MANY GOLFERS PAMPER THEIR TITANIUM-SHAFTED, $750 drivers more than they do their children—and with good reason, by the way. A driver may misbehave (so do kids), it may embarrass you in front of your friends (so do kids), and it may make you regret ever having brought it home (ditto, kids), but a driver will never, ever sass you with impudent back talk.

So it's understandable that golfers love and coddle their drivers and other clubs. That makes them an easy target.

On a steep hill, simply unsnap the cart belt securing the clubs to the cart. The sound of a golf bag falling from a speeding cart is one of the most jarring noises in golf—at least until you realize it wasn't yours. Do this after every time he hits a shot or until he threatens to kill you.

A PENNY GLUED
IS A PENNY STUCK

LIKE A SMALL SHELL OF A POPCORN KERNEL, IT'S SO tiny it's almost irrelevant. But if it's impossible to dislodge, it can be very annoying. Super Glue a penny into the inner sole of your partner's shoe. He may not notice it until it starts to drive him mad. If you can't find a penny, remove one tack from the clubhouse bulletin board and use that instead. The reaction will be instantaneous and more fierce.

CAN YOU DIG IT?

EARLY IN THE MORNING, GO OUT WITH A SHOVEL, A strong back, and a cunning mind, and rearrange the hole markers so the course follows an impossibly confusing route that makes about as much convoluted sense as an old Dr. Seuss nursery rhyme.

THE LITTLE YELLOW WIRE

EVERY GOLF CART IN THE MODERN WORLD HAS A little yellow wire running from the brake pedal to the actual brakes that, once applied, stops a moving cart and prevents it from running into things like trees, lakes, or other carts. Using wire cutters, snip it. Pandemonium will ensue. This is a prank you can do only once.

BALLS AWAY!

PRETEND TO BE A GOOD GUY AND TELL YOUR BUDDY you'll pay for the range balls, then do so. Try to set the bucket on top of a really steep hill that has a long asphalt path leading straight to where they park all the Cadillacs. Then take wire cutters and carefully snip the vertical wires around the bottom of the cage (use scissors if it's a cloth bag). When he picks up the bag, the entire contents will spill out like water from a bottomless bucket. Everyone will have a good laugh as your buddy scrambles down the hill trying to stop

about one hundred range balls from dinging a parking lot full of luxury cars. Well, almost everyone.

SPRING FORWARD

IN YOUR EVIL-DEEDS WORKSHOP, RIG A SPRING SO IT will set to detonate seconds after it is jarred or when the slightest weight lands on it. Then routinely offer to tend the flag. When his ball is close enough for a certain sinker, remove the flag and put the loaded spring into the cup. Seconds after the ball hits the bottom of the cup—look out—it'll come erupting up out of the hole like Ol' Faithful, perhaps blackening an eye or (cross your fingers) replacing one. Who knows? Maybe someday he'll thank you. A Titleist winking out of an empty eye socket is pretty cool.

Seconds after the ball hits
the bottom of the cup—look out—
it'll come erupting up out of
the hole like Ol' Faithful.

ROLE PLAY

Deep down in the soul of every man and woman there resides a ham, someone eager to sever the bonds of their drab human existence, to blossom into something other than what they've become. At one time or another, every one of us has dreamed of what it would be like to be a movie star, a chameleon unrecognizable even to those who know us best. Some great pranks offer you or others the chance to live out this dream, not on the silver screen, but on the fairway green.

MY GURU,
YOUR NIGHTMARE

INVENT A WACKY, IMAGINARY GURU AND INTRODUCE him to your playing partners. Consult him out loud before each and every shot. Ask questions of yourself like you're confirming what the guru divined, such as: "So you really think this putt's going to break right?" Keep congratulating the guru every time you make a good shot, but the second you hit a bad shot or miss a putt, berate him and dismiss him in humiliating terms. Then invent a new imaginary guru. Do this until your playing partners beg you to cease.

Agree to do so, but then start asking them for advice like they were the imaginary guru, the only one who is aware of the bitter consequences.

Even an imaginary guru will help you concentrate on your golf tasks. Your opponents' rounds will suffer because, with an imaginary guru, things will start feeling a bit crowded to the claustrophobic sorts.

LUNATIC GREENSKEEPER

TELL YOUR PARTNERS YOU HEARD THE GREENSKEEPER was recently released from a mental institute where he'd been sent after having a breakdown over job-related stress. Then pay someone to wear dark overalls and have him act like a maniac every time one of you takes a divot, doesn't repair a ball mark, or lets the cart tires drift into the fairway.

PLAY FAIR

HIRE A MAN IN A WHITE SMOCK TO GIVE FREE ON-course club testing. Have him rig up a phony little test and declare all your clubs legal and all your opponents' illegal, according to USGA standards. If your opponent continues to use the fraudulent clubs, insist he give you multiple strokes.

A NOT-SO-
SECRET-SERVICE

HIRE A PRESIDENTIAL LOOK-ALIKE AND SECRET Service entourage and book them the tee time right before your own. Have the jaunty Commander-in-Chief glad-hand with the public before teeing off and then have him play one of the slowest, most miserable rounds ever witnessed on a golf course.

Most Americans, Republican or Democrat, would be thrilled to spend time on the same golf course with the most powerful person in the world. But with golfers, that thrill will evaporate after about one hole of slow play. Then most of the guys in your foursome will become infuriated that the president is taking multiple mulligans, strolling aimlessly without a club, and spending upwards of fifteen minutes looking for lost balls.

That's when the real fun begins. Most golfers won't be able to help themselves and will start shouting at the prez to get a move on.

This won't sit well with the burly men who've been hired to pose as Secret Service agents. Have them become warlike in their defense of the POTUS.

By the fourth or fifth hole, you ought to be able to goad your buddies into actually hitting into the President of the United States. Ah, the power of golf.

HIGH-AND-DRY

PAY AN OVERALL-WEARING GREENS SUPERINTENDENT to shadow your foursome and turn the sprinkler system to "Flood" every time your victim's ball approaches a sprinkler head. If the victim, dripping wet, comes to complain about the repeated soakings, make sure your belligerent accomplice snarls, "Look! I'm just doing my job! You should be grateful you get to play golf while guys like me are working to see that you have a nice time!"

FLIRT FOR HIRE

THE GOOD-NATURED GIRLS WHO DRIVE THE CARTS are usually so bored out of their minds they'll happily play a role in a good-natured prank. For $20, they'll play it with relish.

Give the drink-cart girl an advance tip to shower your victim with affectionate attention. He'll be flattered at first, overjoyed even. But as she continues to focus on him and him alone, his game will fall apart. Have her goad him into hitting impossible shots over distant trees and lakes. He, of course, will gamely try and fail.

Once this happens, have her role switch from cooing support to outright ridicule. "What kind of man are you?" she'll sneer. "And to think I thought of giving you my phone number!"

MARSHALL FOR HIRE

THIS IS THE PSYCHOTIC REVERSE OF THE ABOVE. Instead of flattery, employ fear. The role of marshall may usually fall to paunchy, retired old men, but on a golf course, they carry the same weight as old

Marshall Matt Dillon from *Gunsmoke*. You don't want to cross a marshall. Even young, impudent golfers must respect the marshall.

Use this to your advantage. Pay the marshall $20 to be friendly and amiable to everyone in your group and have him focus on one member of your group with withering scrutiny.

For every "Nice shot!" he gives you, have him give two "You're holding everyone up with your constant waggling! Move it! Move it! Move it!" to your exasperated buddy.

After two or three holes of this haranguing, have him shake his head and start muttering into a walkietalkie. Bonus points if you can talk the marshall into bringing another cart-rover into the fray to ratchet up the heat.

DIVINE INTERVENTIONS

PAY THE GROUP AHEAD TO LAY IN WAIT ON BLIND holes and steal drives struck right down the middle. When your buddy gets fed up, have him angrily accuse the miscreants of petty theft. Ready for this, have the group take umbrage and announce that they are a group of visiting clergy and would never stoop to such unholy antics and that there must be some explanation. Men of God would never stoop to thievery, for Heaven's sake.

This will surely soothe ruffled feathers. Hands will be shook, hard feelings will soften, and the game will resume.

Then, on the next hole, have one of the self-professed clergymen dash from behind a tree and steal a ball in plain sight.

A TRUE
SKINS GAME

GET THE GUYS IN THE PRO SHOP TO PLAY ALONG. Have them put up a sign or two saying that next Wednesday is "Speedo Day." Any golfer who shows up to golf in a Speedo gets to play free! Have them remove the signs so only your mark is targeted.

Convince your target that, man, what a great deal that is and, damn the torpedoes, you're going to do it!

Then don't and hope he does.

Have the pro shop guys put
up a sign or two saying that next
Wednesday is "Speedo Day."

STICKY
FINGERS

PURCHASE A COMMON SHIRT, HAT AND OTHER CLUB logo goodies from the pro shop and leave all the tags on. Then, a few weeks later, plant the items in your mark's bag. Tell the pro he's a kleptomaniac and that you saw him steal a shirt. Tell the pro to check his bag. Do it with him.

Tell the pro you're sorry. You've seen it all before. Tell him his psychologist advises him to be strongly confronted—and to expect some strong denials.

Then sit back and watch the fun.

NEXT ON
THE TEE . . .

BOOK A PREDAWN TEE TIME AND ARRANGE WITH THE pro shop to ask, as is custom, for each player's name upon arrival. Then have them ask for the spelling. Have them say, "Well, we don't have that here. We'll get you in."

After an hour or so, casually show up and apologize for being late. Your partners will say there's been some mistake and that they have no tee time. Promise you'll straighten it out.

Come back out and say they'd spelled the name, say, Miller, with an additional "l" like "Milller" and that they apologized for the error.

This is a minor prank, barely worthy of inclusion amidst truly devious stunts, but it'll buy you an extra hour of sleep and your friends will tee off in a highly agitated state.

WHEN THE GOING GETS TOUGH

Let's face it. Even armed with some of the greatest and most diabolical practical jokes ever dreamed up, you can't win 'em all. Sometimes you're simply outgunned and overmatched by a more skillful opponent. For some, that's when it's time to admit defeat, the fools.

For a practical joker, that's when it's time to get really creative.

FAKE YOUR OWN DEATH

IF ALL YOUR STUNTS, PRANKS, AND SKILLS FAIL TO overcome a worthy opponent and it looks like your match will end badly, it may be time to fake your own death. Even the most cutthroat golfer will have to become somewhat sympathetic when you start clutching your heart and wheezing, "I'm gonna finish this match if it kills me!"

This is another very childish prank, but it'll work and either get you out of the match or at least buy you some strokes down the stretch—that is if you don't suffer a real stroke down the stretch.

FAKE YOUR OWN DEATH
IN TECHNICOLOR

SPEND THE MORNING COMPLAINING LOUDLY ABOUT a disagreeable ethnic meal you'd consumed the night before. Say you'd heard rumors that the country of origin was being overrun by an exotic virus that consumes people in minutes from the inside out, but that your cheap wife persuaded you to go because she had a coupon. When it's clear all is lost, find an on-course restroom, dash in, and begin moaning.

Gradually escalate the moans until you're screaming in agony. Then before becoming absolutely silent, remove your shoes, climb over the wall of the stall and out the rear window. Flee the course, leaving only your shoes behind. Bonus points if you have stashed an open gallon of tomato juice to splash around the seat and into the bowl.

This is to be used only when a match is hopelessly lost and you need a face-saving maneuver to get out of paying up.

SECURE YOUR OWN DEATH

MANY LATE, BELOVED GOLFERS HAVE EXPIRED because they weren't sufficiently fearful of the awful and beautiful power of lightning.

True: The National Severe Storms Laboratory in Norman, Oklahoma, says it developed its lightning-awareness motto so it would be understood by both four-year-old toddlers and inebriated adult golfers. The motto?

If you see it, flee it. If you hear it, fear it.

Good advice, and something you should ignore if the

When things look grim,
grab a long, low iron and begin
running around the fairway.

match and your loot are in jeopardy. When things look grim, both on the scorecard and up in the heavens, grab a long, low iron and begin running around the fairway with it raised toward the heavens, yelling, "I'd rather die than lose!"

Be warned: This is extremely life-threatening behavior, and it could end up costing you your life. Of course, that would result in you having a few more bucks to bestow on your grieving loved ones, so it's sort of a toss-up.

ARRIVEDERCI, SOURPUSS!

Most people have a sense of humor, God bless 'em. It's been said that a boy or girl has never really grown up until they've learned to laugh at themselves. Of course, if you can't laugh at someone else, what fun is it having them around? For those serious sorts, there are some ways to say goodbye and good riddance in style.

A REAL HONEY OF A PRANK

THROUGHOUT THE ROUND, FIND WAYS TO PUT LITTLE dabs of honey on your opponent's hat, his shoes, his shirt—everywhere. Then during a crucial hole in the match, pull a jar full of angry bees from your bag, shake them, and turn them loose.

Remember: Always put little holes in the jar lid so the little bees can breathe. Doing otherwise would risk you being labeled cruel. Well, even more cruel than someone who would loose a hive of angry bees on one honey of an unsuspecting golfer.

ASHES TO ASHES, DUST TO DIVOTS

TAKE SOME OLD ASHES FROM THE FIREPLACE AND PUT them in a ceremonial vase inscribed with "Uncle Ben" in decorative script. Bring them to your next match.

Inform your opponent that these are the mortal remains of your beloved Uncle Ben, the man who taught you everything you know about golf. It is your intention to sprinkle the ashes around the course, one of Uncle Ben's favorites, so he'll be forever connected to a place where you and he shared so many great memories.

Sprinkle some on the right side of the first tee and say, "This is the spot from which he always chose to drive his long, elegant tee shots."

Farther on down the fairway, sprinkle a small amount and say, "He once hit a six iron over the trees to within three feet of the flag from this spot."

Dump some on the green and say it's the spot from which he once sunk a long putt. Commemorate bunkers, trees, streams, hills, knolls at least four times per hole. Do this so excessively and so reverentially that it starts to creep out your opponent (he'll probably be pretty creeped out by the whole thing anyway). Push it so far he'll gently ask you to curb your memorials for, perhaps, a more private time.

Thunder with indignant outrage, "How dare you! Uncle Ben was my best friend! He meant more to me than anyone on earth! He was always there for me! Why, if he was here right now, he'd slap you for your impudence!"

Turn thoughtful for a moment, slowly nod, then heave the remaining ashes right in the guy's kisser.

OUTER LIMITS

TELL OPPONENTS YOU LEARNED A MAGIC SWING THAT allows you to hit fifty yards farther than their best drive. Tell them you learned it from an Indian mystic and can only use it once a month or so or it's straight off to the chiropractor.

Explain that if they hit a drive three hundred yards, yours will be at least fifty yards farther. Make it simple. You both hit from the same spot. His drive goes three hundred yards, and yours will be at least fifty yards farther. You'll even use one of their balls, rather than your own. All legitimate, all within the rules. But with a special swing.

Let them hit first. If they don't hit a good drive, let them hit another. Heck, let them hit until they're satisfied—say, best of ten.

When it's finally your turn to hit, approach the ball the way you normally do. Then step straight over the ball, turn, and face the exact opposite direction. Belt one. Even if you dub it, guaranteed, it'll still be at least fifty yards farther than their ball.

Offer to wait there if they want to pace it off. It'll

really sting if you make the offer after you've hit the ball into a deep lake behind the tee.

AN ATTRACTIVE GOLFER

INSERT POWERFUL INDUSTRIAL MAGNETS IN YOUR putter and two balls you use solely for the putting green. Amaze your opponents by automatically retrieving balls with the push of a button. Explain to the more simple-minded members of your foursome that it's all the power of your mind.

You can't do it on the course—yet. But you are feverishly working on it, and a breakthrough is imminent. Tell them you can bend forks and are working on bending golf clubs. When one player's not looking, remove his putter from his bag and put a nasty bend in it over your knee. Replace it. When he notices it cannot be used and comes screaming after you, deny it. They will spend the rest of the day wondering if you can or cannot use your mind for such dark purposes. Occasionally stare at each player with a cold, penetrating gaze.

A TRULY
"BOOMING" DRIVE

YOU'LL ONLY GET TO DO THIS ONE ONCE, SO MAKE sure you time it impeccably. As your opponent prepares to line up an important drive, place a lit fire-cracker down the back of his pants. Make sure it's far enough below the belt that he can't free it before it explodes. Then run and duck behind a tree.

HANG
'EM HIGH

WHILE YOUR OPPONENT'S CART IS PARKED UNDER a convenient limb, loop fishing line around several club heads. Throw the line over the limb and secure it to the golf cart. When he merrily drives the cart away, the clubs will shoot out of the bag and dangle from the tree like defective Christmas ornaments.

ODE D'
BUG SPRAY

PRIOR TO THE ROUND ON A HOT SUMMER DAY, SWAP the contents of your bug spray with some cheap, eye-stinging perfume. Complain on the first hole about the swarms of bugs that are stinging you or otherwise distracting you from solid golf. Then while your opponent is hitting, make a show of "spraying" yourself with some effective bug spray. Pronounce yourself satisfied that the bug spray is satisfactory.

Then turn to your victim and ask, "Want some?"

He'll be grateful when you toss him the bottle and will proceed to luxuriously coat his arms, legs, neck, and face with "Cheap Harlot No. 5," some of the nastiest perfume known to man. This, in and of itself, will be uproariously funny.

It'll get even funnier when he learns perfumes actually attract, rather than repel, bees and mosquitoes and other winged nastiness.

SLICK MOVE

WHILE YOUR OPPONENT IS GETTING A HOT DOG, using the restroom or searching for a ball deep in the woods, cover everything he'll touch—grips, balls, cart steering wheel, with a thin layer of vaseline. Don't plan on golfing with this person ever again.

FROM THE BIG TOP TO THE BIG PLOP

WHEN THE CIRCUS IS IN TOWN, LURE ONE OF THE elephants out to the golf course. Prior to the round, go to the local feed store and buy a truckload of Elephant Chow. Mix it with a kiddie pool-sized tub of Ex-Lax. Timing could be tricky, but try to work it so the mighty beast's bowels erupt right on the 18th green and right on your buddy's match-winning birdie putt, thus guaranteeing you a victory that will be covered in the following day's newscasts and in any historic discussion about great pranks throughout history.

How do you lure an elephant away from the circus to the golf course and get it to do your bidding? That's up to you.

The title of this book is *Golf's Greatest Practical Jokes*, not *How to Steal an Elephant*.

Timing could be tricky, but try to work it so the mighty beast's bowels erupt right on the 18th green.